# TURTLE CROSSING

*Rick Chrustowski*

Henry Holt and Company

New York

Henry Holt and Company, LLC
*Publishers since 1866*
175 Fifth Avenue
New York, New York 10010
www.henryholtchildrensbooks.com

Henry Holt® is a registered trademark of
Henry Holt and Company, LLC.
Copyright © 2006 by Rick Chrustowski
Distributed in Canada by H. B. Fenn and Company Ltd.

Library of Congress Cataloging-in-Publication Data

Chrustowski, Rick.
Turtle crossing / Rick Chrustowski.—1st ed.
    p.          cm.
    ISBN-13: 978-0-8050-7498-7 / ISBN-10: 0-8050-7498-8
    1. Painted turtle—Life cycles—Juvenile literature.  I. Title.
QL666.C547C47 2006
597.92'592—dc22
                                    2005012169

First Edition—2006
The artist used up to forty layers of colored pencil over
watercolor wash on 140-pound watercolor paper
to create the illustrations for this book.
Printed in the United States of America on acid-free paper. ∞

10  9  8  7  6  5  4  3  2  1

*Special thanks to Madeleine Linck at Three Rivers Park District*

When the first spring rain trickles through the soil, a baby painted turtle comes to life in an underground nest. She claws her way up through mud and tangled roots, out of the darkness into dazzling light.

Soon her brothers and sisters scramble out of the nest and begin the march to find water. The little female leads them through a field and stops in the tall grass at the edge of a road. She stretches her neck and sniffs the air. The scent of water is strong. In a burst of energy, she skitters across the pavement, slides down a sandy bank, and plops into the cool, green water of a pond. Safe!

The turtle is the size of a quarter. Her shell is soft and doesn't protect her yet. She spends the summer alone, hiding in the shadows near the water's edge. *Chomp. Chomp.* Her jaws clamp shut on a wriggling beetle larva. *Gulp!* Underwater, the turtle is quick and graceful. She is a deadly predator to the minnows, tadpoles, and water bugs she chases down.

The pond is also home to other predators. An ancient snapping turtle prowls the murky water. His shell is bigger than a bicycle helmet. His crushing jaws gobble any animal that crosses his path. Luckily, he never notices the little turtle as she darts under leaves. The snapper is hunting larger prey.

The painted turtle peeks out of her shell just in time to see the monstrous reptile block out the sun before he disappears into the deep.

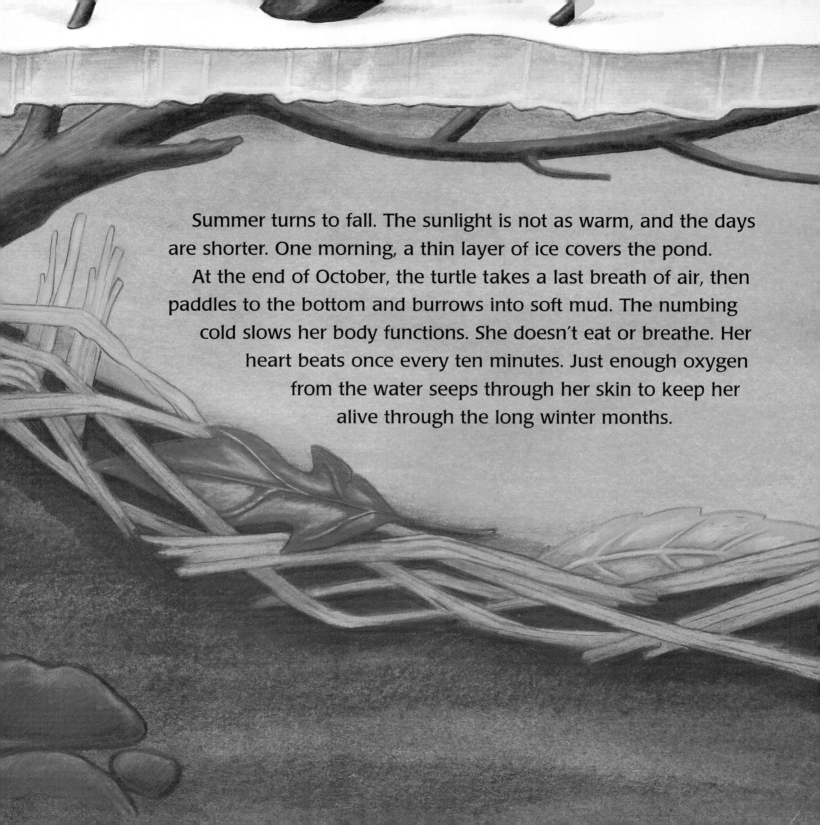

Summer turns to fall. The sunlight is not as warm, and the days are shorter. One morning, a thin layer of ice covers the pond.

At the end of October, the turtle takes a last breath of air, then paddles to the bottom and burrows into soft mud. The numbing cold slows her body functions. She doesn't eat or breathe. Her heart beats once every ten minutes. Just enough oxygen from the water seeps through her skin to keep her alive through the long winter months.

    Finally, in March, sunlight filters through the ice and dances across the bottom of the pond. The turtle stretches one foot out of the mud, then pulls her body free.

    Now she floats at the surface, gulping fresh air into her lungs for the first time in almost six months. Before she can eat, the turtle needs to warm up. She finds the perfect spot to perch and soak up some rays: on top of the shell of one of her neighbors.

The turtle spends summer days basking in the sun. In fall, she gets ready for winter. And in spring, it is time to grow strong again.

Each year a new ridge forms around her shell. When she is five years old, her shell is so tough that few predators can harm her.

At this stage in her life, the turtle feels an urge even stronger than survival. A male turtle feels it, too. He swims close enough to touch her. At last, she notices him.

The turtles chase through winding stems of water lilies. The male glides ahead, then spins around to face the female. He touches his nose to hers and flutters his long, curved claws across her cheeks. When she touches his feet with her claws, they sink to the bottom to mate.

A month later, in June, the female turtle hauls her heavy body out of the water to look for a place to dig a nest. The perfect spot lies on the other side of a road. It's the same field where she was born.

Her belly scrapes against the pavement as she makes her way across. Cars often zip back and forth, but she reaches the other side safely.

At the top of a small hill, the turtle scoops dirt away with her hind feet. Then she tips the back end of her shell into the hole and lays five leathery eggs. After the last one drops in, she buries the nest and tamps it down with her belly to hide it from hungry skunks and raccoons.

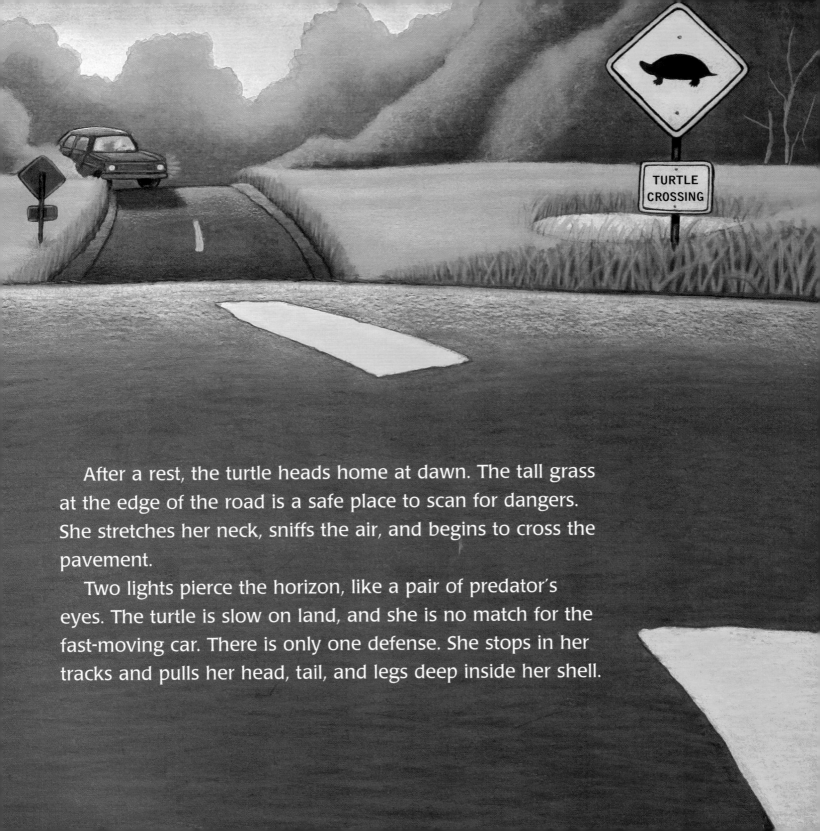

After a rest, the turtle heads home at dawn. The tall grass at the edge of the road is a safe place to scan for dangers. She stretches her neck, sniffs the air, and begins to cross the pavement.

Two lights pierce the horizon, like a pair of predator's eyes. The turtle is slow on land, and she is no match for the fast-moving car. There is only one defense. She stops in her tracks and pulls her head, tail, and legs deep inside her shell.

The lights grow brighter as the car speeds closer. Just when its shadow reaches the turtle, the car stops. The doors open, and two people step out.

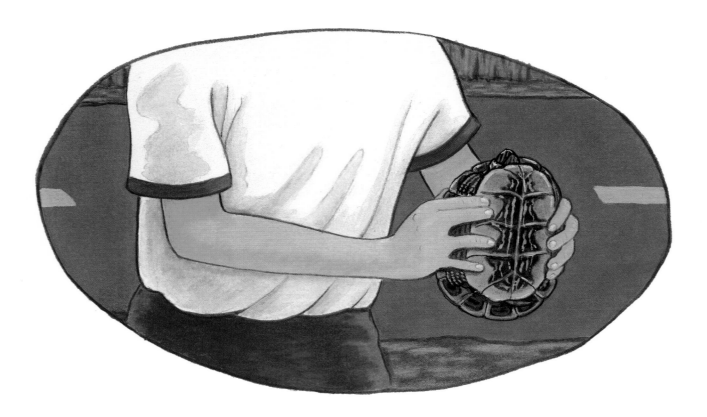

While his mother watches for traffic, a boy picks up the turtle. He carries her across the road and sets her down on the side she was heading toward.

The turtle stays inside her shell. But when she sees the water, she pops her head and legs out and rushes into the pond.

When the turtle comes to the surface again, the car is gone.
As quickly as they entered her life, the people disappeared.
Her eggs are safely hidden in the field across the road. And
now she is safe, too, at home in the pond.

The turtle climbs onto a log and stretches her neck and legs. Sunlight seeps into her shell and warms her striped skin from the tip of her nose to the toes on her webbed feet.

In spring, her babies will claw their way out of the earth. She might never see them. But some of them will make it across the road to hide in the cattails until they are large enough to leave the pond and lay eggs of their own.

# TURTLE TRAFFIC

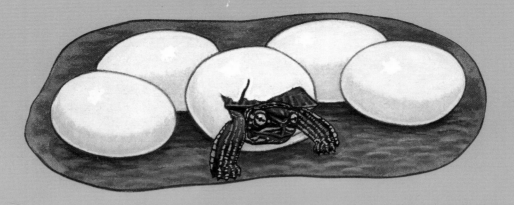

Why did the turtle cross the road? Chances are she was on her way to a nesting site. From May through June, female painted turtles leave the safety of their watery home in search of places to lay their eggs. They lay four to ten eggs in boot-shaped chambers that they dig into dry earth. The baby turtles hatch three to three and a half months later. In northern regions, baby turtles hatch but stay buried in their nests until spring. Their bodies are suspended in a supercooled state like hibernation. They don't need food or water during this period. When winter is finally over, they leave the nest.

Because turtles are cold-blooded reptiles, they need to absorb heat from their environment. They can be seen basking in the sun on rocks or on logs in ponds, lakes, rivers, and marshes across North America. They eat snails, leeches, fish, insects, water plants, and frogs.

The painted turtle is named for the brightly colored patterns that look as though they were painted on its plastron (bottom shell). The carapace (top shell) is either olive or brown with dark markings to help the turtle blend in with its surroundings.

Turtles have an effective method of defense. When in danger, a turtle pulls its head, tail, and legs into its hard shell to keep safe. The shell is actually a fusion of the turtle's spine and ribs. The outer shell is covered by scutes, which are similar to human toenails. Few predators can break through an adult turtle shell.

Young turtles have softer shells. They can be eaten by raccoons, skunks, herons, foxes, and even large fish. If a turtle can make it through the first four or five years, its shell will have grown strong. Then it can live into its twenties or longer.

Each year thousands of turtles don't make it across the road. Many are run over by speeding cars. Where turtle traffic is high, some park departments put up TURTLE CROSSING signs during egg-laying season.

All turtles can bite, although most will hide in their shell when approached. But some types, like snapping turtles, can cause injury to people and should be handled with extreme caution. The best way to help a turtle found in the road is to first make sure there is no danger from oncoming traffic, then put it on the side that it was heading toward.